I Must Confess

31 Daily Declarations of God's Promises for You and Your Family

Phil: 4:6-8

Marx Succès Sr.

Life to Legacy, LLC

I Must Confess: 31 Daily Declarations of God's Promises for You and Your Family

By: Marx Succès

ISBN-13 978-1-939654-43-4
ISBN-10 1939654432

Printed in the United States

10 9 8 7 6 5 4 3 2 1

www.life2legacy.com

Book and Cover Design by Forerunners Ink LLC

Presented to:

Evan. Dorfredia

God Bless you

thank you

so much

To contact the author, send an e-mail to:
mmsucces@yahoo.com

DEDICATION

I dedicate my first book to my wonderful wife, Marie, God's gift to me for the last twenty-six years. You have been an inspiration and source of strength for me over the years. I also dedicate this book to my two beautiful children, Marx Jr. and Maria. I am so proud of you and your walk with God. Thank you for being the best son and daughter a father can ask for. I also want to thank my spiritual father and mother in the faith, Bishop Carlis L. Moody Sr. and Mother Mary Moody. My family and I love you and appreciate you very much. Last but not least, to my mother and father, Gaspard and Marcelle Succès: Thank you for sacrificing so much to bring me to America from Haiti in 1977 at the age of ten. This was all in God's plan for my life. Love you all.

Foreword

Elder Marx Succès was born in the midst of poverty in Port-Au-Prince, Haiti. The desire for a better life for the family brought his parents to America. At the age of ten, he was brought to America by his grandparents to live with his parents, where he could receive an education. His parents were not aware of God's call upon his life. After finishing high school, he attended Northern Illinois University, where he received a bachelor's degree in physical education. He also attended Olivet Nazarene University, where he received a master's degree in curriculum and instruction, and a master's degree in school administration. At the end of his last school year, God's purpose and plan for his life came into action; he received Christ as Savior and was baptized in the Holy Ghost.

The Lord has blessed Elder Succès with the spirit of fasting and prayer. From those times of prayer and fasting, the Lord has led him to encourage the saints by writing this devotional. It is a faith devotional for everyday reading. It can be used along with your prayer time. I recommend this devotional to you.

Bishop Carlis L. Moody Sr.
Faith Temple Church of God in Christ, Pastor
Church of God in Christ International President of Home/ Foreign Missions Department

INTRODUCTION

There's a Scripture in the Bible that is often quoted but rarely practiced: "Death and life are in the power of the tongue, and they that love it shall eat the fruit thereof" (Proverbs 18:21). Most Christians underestimate the power of the spoken Word. One of the biggest lies that has ever been told comes in the form of a slogan we have been repeating for generations. And it goes like this: "Sticks and stones may break my bones, but words will never hurt me."

A broken bone will heal much faster than hurtful words that are imbedded deep in our hearts. The truth of the matter is that negative words, declarations, and confessions can form and shape your destiny. Many people have confessed and spoken curses over their lives, over their families and their children, instead of confessing and declaring what the Word of God says. Oftentimes, people look at their families and their children in their present state and, because of anger and disappointment, will allow satan to let them speak negative things over their lives. I'm here to tell you today that you don't have to wait for things to get better in your life or your families' lives before you start declaring the blessings and promises of God over them. Listen to the words of Romans 4:17: "As it is written, I have made thee a father of many nations, before him whom he believed, even God, who quickeneth the dead, and calleth those things which be not as though they were." God calls those things that are not as though they were. Even in our state of imperfection and shortcomings, God's thoughts of us are thoughts of peace and not evil, to give us a hope and a future. In the first chapter of the book of Job, God told satan that Job was a perfect and upright man, even though in the latter chapters we discover that Job had many issues that God had to deal with.

James teaches us a valuable lesson about the tongue. The tongue is one of the most powerful weapons that we have at our disposal to help us fight this good fight of faith. The tongue is a weapon that can be used for good or for evil. Consider James's definition of a perfect man: "One that does not offend in speech (never says the wrong things)." The only way not to say the wrong things is to say what the Bible says. Hallelujah! James also declares:

> 2 For we all often stumble and fall and offend in many things. And if anyone does not offend in speech [never says the wrong things], he is a fully developed character and a perfect man, able to control his whole body and to curb his entire nature.
> 3 If we set bits in the horses' mouths to make them obey us, we can turn their whole bodies about.
> 4 Likewise, look at the ships: though they are so great and are driven by rough winds, they are steered by a very small rudder wherever the impulse of the helmsman determines.
> 5 Even so the tongue is a little member, and it can boast of great things. See how much wood or how great a forest a tiny spark can set ablaze!
> 6 And the tongue is a fire. [The tongue is a] world of wickedness set among our members, contaminating and depraving the whole body and setting on fire the wheel of birth (the cycle of man's nature), being itself ignited by hell (Gehenna).
> 7 For every kind of beast and bird, of reptile and sea animal, can be tamed and has been tamed by human genius (nature).
> 8 But the human tongue can be tamed by no man. It is a restless (undisciplined, irreconcilable) evil, full of deadly poison.

9 With it we bless the Lord and Father, and with it
we curse men who were made in God's likeness!
10 Out of the same mouth come forth blessing
and cursing. These things, my brethren, ought
not to be so.
11 Does a fountain send forth [simultaneously]
from the same opening fresh water and bitter?
12 Can a fig tree, my brethren, bear olives, or a
grapevine figs? Neither can a salt spring furnish
fresh water. (**James 3:2-12, AMP**)

I have a saying that I often repeat: "If I'm going to have what I say, I might as well say what the Bible says."

This is why the Lord has given me charge to write a book to empower and equip the saints in the fight for their families. He instructed me to write a book that can be used over and over again. So this is not a one-and-done book. This is a thirty-one-day devotional book that can be repeated every month for the rest of your life. Because it is the confession of the pure, unadulterated Word of God, it will never get old, boring, or out of date. The writer of Hebrews declares:

> For the Word that God speaks is alive and full of power [making it active, operative, energizing, and effective]; it is sharper than any two-edged sword, penetrating to the dividing line of the breath of life (soul) and [the immortal] spirit, and of joints and marrow [of the deepest parts of our nature], exposing and sifting and analyzing and judging the very thoughts and purposes of the heart. (**Hebrews 4:12, AMP**)

It is my prayer that you will confess these Scriptures and prayers several times daily, and commit them to memory. Use this God-inspired devotional as a tool and a weapon to reshape the destiny of your family and—by faith—see it bring blessings upon your generations.

JOSHUA 1:8

This book of the law shall not depart out of thy mouth; but thou shalt meditate therein day and night, that thou mayest observe to do according to all that is written therein: for then thou shalt make thy way prosperous, and then thou shalt have good success.

Get ready for GOOD SUCCESS in every area of your lives!

SPECIAL NOTES:

- I've left blank spaces in the confessions for you to write in the names of your family. *(Optional)*
- I've also included several blank pages throughout the book for you to record your testimonials, because I am one hundred percent confident that, as you confess the Word and pray these prayers, you will see changes and positive results and experience signs, wonders, and miracles in your life and in the lives of your family members.

Opening Prayer

Pray this opening prayer as you begin your journey of *I Must Confess*:

> *Father, I come to you in the name of my Lord and Savior Jesus Christ. I thank you, Father, that I can come boldly to your throne of grace as a child of the Most High God, to obtain mercy and find grace to help me in my time of need. Thank you, Father, for your Word, which is alive and active. Father, please forgive me for every negative word, every word of doubt and unbelief that I've ever spoken out of my mouth. I renounce them right now in the name of Jesus. They shall not take root and prosper over my life or over the lives of any member of my family. From this day forward, I will speak and confess your word and your promises that are in the Bible. Father, you said in Isaiah 55:11: "So shall my word be that goeth forth out of my mouth: it shall not return unto me void, but it shall accomplish that which I please, and it shall prosper in the thing whereto I sent it." As I start this journey of daily confessing your Word and your promises over my life and over the lives of my family, I declare this day that your word will go out and accomplish everything that it is supposed to accomplish. I declare that our lives will never be the same. The words that will be spoken out of my mouth from this day forward will bring glory, honor, and praise to your name. I confess this in the name of Jesus Christ of Nazareth, AMEN!*

Day 1

THE SCRIPTURE

"And the LORD thy God will circumcise thine heart, and the heart of thy seed, to love the LORD thy God with all thine heart, and with all thy soul, that thou mayest live."

Deuteronomy 30:6

THE CONFESSION

Father, in the name of Jesus, I thank you and praise you for this divine promise. I declare today that my heart and the heart of my seed (children) have been circumcised. I declare that not only do I love you with all of my heart, all of my soul, all of my mind, and all of my strength, but I also declare that my seed (insert names)______________________ love you with all of their hearts, souls, minds, and strengths. I declare that my seed shall not be cut off before their time, but "they shall live" and fulfill your will and purpose for their lives. I confess this in the name of Jesus Christ of Nazareth, AMEN!

Throughout the Day

Thank you Lord, that all of my children are saved.
Thank you Lord, that my children are in your perfect will.
Thank you Lord, that my family has found favor in your sight.

Day 2

THE SCRIPTURE

"I have been young, and now am old; yet have I not seen the righteous forsaken, nor his seed begging bread. He is ever merciful, and lendeth; and his seed is blessed."

Psalm 37:25-26

THE CONFESSION

Father, in the name of Jesus, I thank you for your word, which is eternally settled in heaven. I stand today on this divine promise and declare that my family and I shall never be forsaken because we stand righteous in your sight. We are the righteousness of God through our Lord and Savior Jesus Christ. I declare today that my seed ______________________________ shall never beg for bread. Father, thank you that we are merciful and we are lenders and not borrowers. Father, thank you that my seed is blessed. I confess this in the name of Jesus Christ of Nazareth, AMEN!

Throughout the Day

Thank you Lord, that my seed shall never be forsaken.
Thank you Lord, that my seed is forever blessed.
Thank you Lord, that we are lenders and not borrowers.

DAY 3

THE SCRIPTURE

"But the mercy of the LORD is from everlasting to everlasting upon them that fear him, and his righteousness unto children's children."

Psalm 103:17

THE CONFESSION

Father, in the name of Jesus, I thank you for your grace and mercy. Thank you that your mercies are new every morning. I thank you for this divine promise today. I declare according to your Word that your mercy is extended to me and my family, from everlasting to everlasting, because we fear you. Thank you that your righteousness extends to my children ______________________________________and my children's children ______________________________ __________. I declare that my children shall be righteous. I declare that my children's children shall be righteous. I confess this in the name of Jesus Christ of Nazareth, AMEN!

THROUGHOUT THE DAY

Thank you Lord, that your mercy is upon me and my family. Thank you Lord, that your righteousness is upon my children's children.

Day 4

THE SCRIPTURE

"Praise ye the LORD. Blessed is the man that feareth the LORD, that delighteth greatly in his commandments. His seed shall be mighty upon earth: the generation of the upright shall be blessed."

Psalm 112:1-2

THE CONFESSION

Father, in the name of Jesus, I thank you for your rich, wonderful blessings that you've bestowed upon me and my family. I thank you for this divine promise today. I declare that my family and I are blessed because we fear you and delight greatly in your commandments. I declare today that my seed ________________________________ shall be mighty upon the earth. Father, I thank you that according to your word, my entire generation shall be blessed. I confess this in the name of Jesus Christ of Nazareth, AMEN!

Throughout the Day

Thank you Lord, that my family and I fear and reverence you and delight greatly in your commandments.

Thank you Lord, that my seed shall be mighty upon the earth.

Thank you Lord, that my generations shall be blessed.

Day 5

THE SCRIPTURE

"The LORD shall increase you more and more, you and your children. Ye are blessed of the LORD which made heaven and earth."
Psalm 115:14-15

THE CONFESSION

Father, in the name of Jesus, I praise and magnify your Holy name. Thank you for your Word, which is quick and powerful and sharper than any two-edged sword. Father, I thank you for this promise today of divine increase. I declare that you are increasing my children ______________________________ ________________ and me, more and more, in every area of our lives. I thank you that we are blessed above and beyond measure because we love, obey, and serve you, the God who made heaven and earth. I confess this in the name of Jesus Christ of Nazareth, AMEN!

THROUGHOUT THE DAY

Thank you Lord, for increasing me and my family in every area of our lives.
Thank you Lord, that we are blessed and highly favored.

TESTIMONIALS

DATE:__________

DATE:__________

DATE:__________

DATE:__________

Day 6

THE SCRIPTURE

"Though hand join in hand, the wicked shall not be unpunished: but the seed of the righteous shall be delivered."
Proverbs 11:21

THE CONFESSION

Father, in the name of Jesus, I thank you and praise you for your goodness and your mercy toward me and my family. Thank you that your word is eternally settled in heaven. Thank you for this divine promise today that my seed____ ________________________________shall be delivered. According to your Word, I speak deliverance from every addiction, every possession and oppression over my entire family in Jesus' name. My family shall no longer be bound, but from this day forward, they are free by the power of God. I confess this in the name of Jesus Christ of Nazareth, AMEN!

Throughout the Day

Thank you Lord, that my seed shall be delivered.
Thank you Lord, that my seed shall not be forgotten.

Day 7

THE SCRIPTURE

"In the fear of the LORD is strong confidence: and his children shall have a place of refuge."
Proverbs 14:26

THE CONFESSION

Father, in the name of Jesus, I thank you for your loving kindness and your tender mercies toward me and my family. I thank you today for this divine promise, and I declare that we fear and reverence your holiness and your righteousness. Thank you for the strong confidence that my family and I have in you as our Lord and King. I confess that my children ______________________________ shall have a place of refuge in you all the days of their lives. I confess this in the name of Jesus Christ of Nazareth, AMEN!

THROUGHOUT THE DAY

Thank you Lord, that my family and I reverence your holy name.
Thank you Lord, that we have strong confidence in you.
Thank you Lord, that my children shall have a place of refuge in you.

Day 8

THE SCRIPTURE

"For I will pour water upon him that is thirsty, and floods upon the dry ground: I will pour my spirit upon thy seed, and my blessing upon thine offspring: And they shall spring up as among the grass, as willows by the water courses."

Isaiah 44:3-4

THE CONFESSION

Father, in the name of Jesus, I thank you for allowing my family and I to see another day. Truly, this is the day that you have made, and we will rejoice and be glad in it. Thank you for this promise on today that you will satisfy our thirsty souls. Father, I confess today that you are pouring out your Spirit upon my seed ________________________________ ______ and your blessings upon my offspring. I declare that they will spring up, grow, prosper and bring glory to your name. I confess this in the name of Jesus Christ of Nazareth, AMEN!

THROUGHOUT THE DAY

Thank you Lord, for pouring your Spirit upon my seed.
Thank you Lord, for pouring your blessings upon my offspring.
Thank you Lord, that my seed shall blossom and prosper in every area of their lives.

Day 9

THE SCRIPTURE

"And all thy children shall be taught of the LORD; and great shall be the peace of thy children."
Isaiah 54:13

THE CONFESSION

Father, in the name of Jesus, I thank you for your word. I thank you, Father, that you honor your word above your name. Thank you for this divine promise on today that all of my children ______________________ are taught of you, and great is their peace. Thank you that my children are filled with your peace, which passes all understanding. Thank you that the godly teaching they've received will never depart from them, but they will hide the word in their hearts and obey the Word all the days of their lives. I confess this in the name of Jesus Christ of Nazareth, AMEN!

THROUGHOUT THE DAY

Thank you Lord, that my children are taught of you. Thank you Lord, that your peace rests, rules, and abides upon me and my family.

Day 10

THE SCRIPTURE

"As for me, this is my covenant with them, saith the LORD; My spirit that is upon thee, and my words which I have put in thy mouth, shall not depart out of thy mouth, nor out of the mouth of thy seed, nor out of the mouth of thy seed's seed, saith the LORD, from henceforth and for ever."

Isaiah 59:21

THE CONFESSION

Father, in the name of Jesus, I thank you for this glorious day that you have made. I declare that I will rejoice and be glad in it. Thank you for this awesome promise for today. I confess today that you are a covenant-keeping God. I confess today that your words will not depart out of my mouth, nor out of the mouths of my children________________________________, nor out of the mouths of my children's children forever. I declare that my generations will honor you and walk in the integrity of your word all the days of their lives. I confess this in the name of Jesus Christ of Nazareth, AMEN!

Throughout the Day

Thank you Lord, that your Spirit is upon me and my family.
Thank you Lord, that your Word shall not depart out of my mouth or the mouths of my family.
Thank you Lord, that we will be doers of your Word and not hearers only.

Testimonials

Date:__________

Date:__________

Date:__________

Date:__________

Day 11

THE SCRIPTURE

"They shall not labour in vain, nor bring forth [children] for trouble; for they are the seed of the blessed of the Lord, and their offspring with them."

Isaiah 65:23 (AMP)

THE CONFESSION

Father, in the name of Jesus, I thank you for being a covenant-keeping God. Thank you, Father, for not breaking your promises. Thank you for this divine promise on today. I declare that according to your word that I will not labor in vain. I declare that I did not bring forth children for trouble. I declare that all of my children____________________ and I are the seed of the blessed of the Lord. I confess this in the name of Jesus Christ of Nazareth, AMEN!

THROUGHOUT THE DAY

Thank you Lord, that my labor has not been in vain.

Thank you Lord, that I have not brought forth children for trouble.

Thank you Lord, that my seed are of you and they are forever blessed.

Day 12

THE SCRIPTURE

"Thou shalt keep therefore his statutes, and his commandments, which I command thee this day, that it may go well with thee, and with thy children after thee, and that thou mayest prolong thy days upon the earth, which the LORD thy God giveth thee, for ever."

Deuteronomy 4:40

THE CONFESSION

Father, in the name of Jesus, I thank you for your Word that is alive and powerful. Thank you that your statutes and commandments that you've instructed me to follow will never depart out of my mouth or the mouths of my children ______________________________. Thank you Lord, that it will go well with my children and me from this day forward and forever. Thank you Lord, that our days shall be prolonged upon the earth. I confess this in the name of Jesus Christ of Nazareth, AMEN!

Throughout the Day

Thank you Lord, that it is well with me and my family.
Thank you Lord, for prolonging our lives.
Thank you Lord, that we keep your statutes and commandments.

Day 13

THE SCRIPTURE

"O that there were such an heart in them, that they would fear me, and keep all my commandments always, that it might be well with them, and with their children for ever!"
Deuteronomy 5:29

THE CONFESSION

Father, in the name of Jesus, I thank you that I can come boldly to your throne of grace. Thank you for this divine promise on today. Thank you Lord, that my heart and the heart of my children____________________ follow after you. Thank you that because we fear and honor you as our God and King it shall be well with us forever. I confess this in the name of Jesus Christ of Nazareth, AMEN!

THROUGHOUT THE DAY

Thank you Lord, that our hearts are pure before you.
Thank you Lord, that all is well with me and my family.
Thank you Lord, for long life, health, and strength.

Day 14

THE SCRIPTURE

"Observe and hear all these words which I command thee, that it may go well with thee, and with thy children after thee for ever, when thou doest that which is good and right in the sight of the LORD thy God."

Deuteronomy 12:28

THE CONFESSION

Father, in the name of Jesus, I thank you for this blessed day. This is the day you have made, and I will rejoice and be glad in it. Thank you for this divine promise on today. Thank you that my family and I observe and keep all of your commandments. Thank you Lord, that it shall be well in every area of our lives because of our obedience to your word. I declare today, that it is well with my children__________________________, it is well with my finances, and it is well with my children's children. I confess this in the name of Jesus Christ of Nazareth, Amen!

Throughout the Day

Thank you Lord, that we observe and keep your word.

Thank you Lord, that all is well with me and my family in every area of our lives.

Thank you Lord, that we do what is good and right in your sight.

Day 15

THE SCRIPTURE

"The secret things belong unto the LORD our God: but those things which are revealed belong unto us and to our children for ever, that we may do all the words of this law."
Deuteronomy 29:29

THE CONFESSION

Father, in the name of Jesus, I thank you that my sins are forgiven and my name is written in your Book of Life. Thank you today for this divine promise. Thank you Lord, for revealing yourself to me and my children____________________________. Thank you for revelation knowledge of you through your Word. Thank you, Lord, that we will be doers of the Word and not hearers only. I confess this in the name of Jesus Christ of Nazareth, Amen!

THROUGHOUT THE DAY

Thank you Lord, for revealing yourself to me and my family.
Thank you Lord, that we are doers of the Word.
Thank you Lord, that we will keep your word forever.

Testimonials

Date:__________

Date:__________

Date:__________

Date:__________

Day 16

THE SCRIPTURE

"I call heaven and earth to record this day against you, that I have set before you life and death, blessing and cursing: therefore choose life, that both thou and thy seed may live."
Deuteronomy 30:19

THE CONFESSION

Father, in the name of Jesus, I thank you for your grace and your mercy toward me and my family. Thank you Lord, for this divine promise today. I declare today that my family and I choose blessings, and we choose the very life of God upon us; therefore, we are blessed and highly favored and we shall live and not die. I confess this in the name of Jesus Christ of Nazareth, AMEN!

THROUGHOUT THE DAY

Thank you Lord, for your blessings upon me and my family.
Thank you Lord, for abundant life on today.
Thank you Lord, that in you we live and breathe and have our very being.

Day 17

THE SCRIPTURE

"What man is he that feareth the LORD? him shall he teach in the way that he shall choose. His soul shall dwell at ease; and his seed shall inherit the earth."

Psalm 25:12-13

THE CONFESSION

Father, in the name of Jesus, I thank you for the entrance of your word that gives light. Thank you for this divine promise on today. Thank you Lord, that I fear and reverence you and your holy name. Thank you Lord, for teaching me in your way. I confess today that my soul dwells at ease and my seed shall inherit the earth. I confess this in the name of Jesus Christ of Nazareth, AMEN!

THROUGHOUT THE DAY

Thank you Lord, for teaching me in your way.
Thank you Lord, that my soul dwells at ease.
Thank you Lord, for divine inheritance in the name of Jesus.

Day 18

THE SCRIPTURE

"Lo, children are an heritage of the LORD: and the fruit of the womb is his reward."

Psalm 127:3

THE CONFESSION

Father, in the name of Jesus, I thank you for another day. Truly this is the day you have made and I declare today that I will rejoice and be glad in it. Thank you for this powerful word on today. Thank you Lord, that my children___________________________________ are good and perfect gifts from you. Thank you Lord, that my children are a heritage from you. Thank you for blessing and rewarding the fruit of my womb. I confess this in the name of Jesus Christ of Nazareth, AMEN!

Throughout the Day

Thank you Lord, for blessing the fruit of my womb.
Thank you Lord, that my children are your perfect gifts to me.
Thank you Lord, for giving me your very best.

Day 19

THE SCRIPTURE

"A good man leaveth an inheritance to his children's children: and the wealth of the sinner is laid up for the just."
Proverbs 13:22

THE CONFESSION

Father, in the name of Jesus, I thank you for your grace and your mercy. Thank you that it is you who gives us the power and the ability and the wisdom to get wealth. Thank you Lord, that everything we have comes from you. I declare that I shall leave an inheritance and a legacy to my children________________________________ and my children's children. I declare that they will prosper physically, financially, emotionally, and spiritually. Thank you Lord, that the wealth of the sinner is laid up for me and my family. I confess this in the name of Jesus Christ of Nazareth, AMEN!

THROUGHOUT THE DAY

Thank you Lord, for a godly inheritance for my children and my children's children.
Thank you Lord, for prospering my generations.
Thank you Lord, that the wealth of the sinner is laid up for me because I am the righteousness of God through Christ Jesus.

Day 20

THE SCRIPTURE

"And I will establish my covenant between me and thee and thy seed after thee in their generations for an everlasting covenant, to be a God unto thee, and to thy seed after thee."

Genesis 17:7

THE CONFESSION

Father, in the name of Jesus I thank you that you are a covenant keeping God and that you have established your covenant between me and my seed____________________ __________ and my future generations as an everlasting covenant between us and you forever. I confess this in the name of Jesus Christ of Nazareth, AMEN!

Throughout the Day

Thank you Lord, for establishing your everlasting covenant with me.

Thank you Lord, for extending your covenant to my seed and my future generations forever.

Thank you Lord, that you are our God and besides you there is no other.

TESTIMONIALS

DATE:__________

DATE:__________

DATE:__________

DATE:__________

Day 21

THE SCRIPTURE

"The just man walketh in his integrity: his children are blessed after him."

Proverbs 20:7

THE CONFESSION

Father, in the name of Jesus, I thank you for saving us and for enabling us to walk in integrity among others, and because of this my children________________________________ are blessed. I declare that we are blessed coming in, and we are blessed going out. I declare that everything we put our hands forth to do is a blessing. I confess this in the name of Jesus Christ of Nazareth, AMEN!

Throughout the Day

Thank you Lord, for the integrity of your word.

Thank you Lord, for justifying me and enabling me to walk in my integrity.

Thank you Lord, for blessing my seed after me.

Day 22

THE SCRIPTURE

"Train up a child in the way he should go: and when he is old, he will not depart from it."
Proverbs 22:6

THE CONFESSION

Father, in the name of Jesus, I thank you for new mercies that I see today. I thank you for my children, whom you have given unto me, and for the wisdom to train them up in your way. Therefore, I confess that my children_________________________________are trained up in the way of the Lord, and when they get old they will not depart from it. They shall forever serve you and walk in your will for their lives. I confess this in the name of Jesus Christ of Nazareth, AMEN!

Throughout the Day

Thank you Lord, for my children.
Thank you Lord, that my children are being trained in your perfect way.
Thank you Lord, that they will not depart from their training when they get old.

Day 23

THE SCRIPTURE

"And it shall come to pass afterward, that I will pour out my spirit upon all flesh; and your sons and your daughters shall prophesy, your old men shall dream dreams, your young men shall see visions."

Joel 2:28

THE CONFESSION

Father, in the name of Jesus, I thank you for being the great I AM. Thank you for the rich, wonderful blessings you've bestowed upon me and my family. I thank you for pouring out your Spirit upon us, my son ________________and my daughter ________________shall prophesy. Thank you Lord, that my children will be used of you and operate in the gifts of Spirit. I confess this in the name of Jesus Christ of Nazareth, AMEN!

THROUGHOUT THE DAY

Thank you Lord, for pouring out your Spirit upon me and my children.

Thank you Lord, that my son and my daughter are prophesying.

Thank you Lord, for giving me dreams and visions.

Day 24

THE SCRIPTURE

"Then Peter said unto them, Repent, and be baptized every one of you in the name of Jesus Christ for the remission of sins, and ye shall receive the gift of the Holy Ghost. For the promise is unto you, and to your children, and to all that are afar off, even as many as the LORD our God shall call."

Acts 2:38-39

THE CONFESSION

Father, in the name of Jesus, I thank you for salvation through the precious blood of Jesus, thank you that I have repented and been baptized in the name of Jesus Christ and that my sins have been remitted and therefore I have received the gift of the Holy Ghost, which is a promise unto me and my children. My son ________________and my daughter ___________________ and my grandchildren and future generations shall receive the promised gift of the Holy Ghost. I confess this in the name of Jesus Christ of Nazareth, AMEN!

Throughout the Day

Thank you Lord, for the remission of my sins and my children's sins.

Thank you Lord, that my children and I have received the promised gift of the Holy Ghost.

Thank you Lord, for including us in your calling.

Day 25

THE SCRIPTURE

"We will not hide them from their children, shewing to the generation to come the praises of the LORD, and his strength, and his wonderful works that he hath done."
Psalm 78:4

THE CONFESSION

Father, in the name of Jesus I thank you that your promises in your Word that you have made known unto us will not be hidden from my children ______________________________. I thank you that my generations to come will be shown your praises, your strength, and all the wonderful works you have done. I confess this in the name of Jesus Christ of Nazareth, AMEN!

THROUGHOUT THE DAY

Thank you Lord, for showing my children and my future generations your praises.
Thank you Lord, that they will see your strength and all the wonderful works you have done.

Testimonials

Date:__________

Date:__________

Date:__________

Date:__________

Day 26

THE SCRIPTURE

"Behold, I and the children whom the LORD hath given me are for signs and for wonders in Israel from the LORD of hosts, which dwelleth in mount Zion."

Isaiah 8:18

THE CONFESSION

Father, in the name of Jesus, I thank you for being God—besides you there is no other. You are the only wise God, and you are all knowing and all powerful. Thank you for this divine promise today. I declare that my children________________________________ and I are for signs and wonders that will bring glory and honor to your name. I declare that others will see your glory shine through us and cry out, "What must I do to be saved?" I confess this in the name of Jesus Christ of Nazareth, AMEN!

THROUGHOUT THE DAY

Thank you Lord, for using me and my family to bring glory to your name.

Thank you Lord, for your hand of protection, which is upon me and my family.

Thank you Lord, for signs and wonders and miracles being manifested in our lives.

Day 27

THE SCRIPTURE

"Thy seed will I establish for ever, and build up thy throne to all generations."

Psalm 89:4

THE CONFESSION

Father, in the name of Jesus, I thank you that you are from everlasting to everlasting and that your truth endures throughout all generations. Thank you for your great and precious promise to establish my seed ______________________________forever and to build up my legacy to all generations. I confess this in the name of Jesus Christ of Nazareth, AMEN!

Throughout the Day

Thank you Lord, for establishing my seed forever

Thank you Lord, that my legacy is built up to all generations.

Day 28

THE SCRIPTURE

"But ye are a chosen generation, a royal priesthood, an holy nation, a peculiar people; that ye should shew forth the praises of him who hath called you out of darkness into his marvellous light."

1 Peter 2:9

THE CONFESSION

Father, in the name of Jesus, I thank you that great is your faithfulness, thank you that you have called my family and I out of darkness into your marvelous light. I thank you Lord, that my family and I are chosen by you, and for making us a royal priesthood, a holy nation, and a peculiar people. I declare that we will show forth your praises and bring glory to your name. I confess this in the name of Jesus Christ of Nazareth, AMEN!

Throughout the Day

Thank you Lord, for making us your royal priesthood.
Thank you Lord, that we are your holy nation.
Thank you Lord, for calling us out of darkness into your marvelous light.

Day 29

THE SCRIPTURE

"Thou shalt know also that thy seed shall be great, and thine offspring as the grass of the earth."
Job 5:25

THE CONFESSION

Father, in the name of Jesus, I will bless you at all times and your praises shall continually be in my mouth. I will boast in you Lord, and the humble shall hear of it and be glad. Thank you for making my seed ______________________________ to be great and my offspring as the grass of the earth. I confess this in the name of Jesus Christ of Nazareth, AMEN!

Throughout the Day

Thank you Lord, for making my seed great.
Thank you Lord, for making my offspring as the grass of the earth.

Day 30

THE SCRIPTURE

"And they said, Believe on the Lord Jesus Christ, and thou shalt be saved, and thy house."
Acts 16:31

THE CONFESSION

Father, in the name of Jesus, I thank you for loving us. I thank you for sending your only begotten son, Jesus Christ, to die for us so that we can be saved. I therefore believe on the Lord Jesus Christ and I am saved, and I declare that my entire household, ______________________________, is also saved. I declare that not one member of my family will die and go to hell, but they will all come into the knowledge of your saving grace. I confess this in the name of Jesus Christ of Nazareth, AMEN!

Throughout the Day

Thank you Lord, that I believe on the Lord Jesus Christ.
Thank you Lord, that I am saved.
Thank you Lord, for saving my entire family.

Day 31

THE SCRIPTURE

"For he established a testimony in Jacob, and appointed a law in Israel, which he commanded our fathers, that they should make them known to their children: That the generation to come might know them, even the children which should be born; who should arise and declare them to their children: That they might set their hope in God, and not forget the works of God, but keep his commandments."

Psalm 78:5-7

THE CONFESSION

Father, in the name of Jesus, I thank you that your law is perfect, converting the soul, and that your testimony is sure, making wise the simple. They are to be desired more than gold and silver, and they are sweeter than the honey and the honeycomb. Lord, I thank you that my children ____________________________ shall know them and teach them to their children and future generations so that they will keep your commandments and set their hope in you and not forget your works. I confess this in the name of Jesus Christ of Nazareth, AMEN!

THROUGHOUT THE DAY

Thank you Lord, for your law, your testimony, and your commandments.

Thank you Lord, that my children know of them and keep them and will teach them to their children.

Thank you Lord, that my children set their hope in you and will not forget your works.

Testimonials

Date:__________

Date:__________

Date:__________

Date:__________

PRAISE FOR "I MUST CONFESS"

"I Must Confess is more than a useful thirty-one-day devotional. God has used Elder Succès to give us a powerful, succinct and relevant resource we can access every day of our lives. When we confess God's word over our lives and over the lives of our children, we are literally speaking the blessings of God, thus fulfilling his will for our lives."

Elder Ed Jackson
Associate Minister, Faith Temple Church of God in Christ
Evanston, Illinois

LIFE TO LEGACY LLC

CPSIA information can be obtained at www.ICGtesting.com
Printed in the USA
LVOW12s1815310515

440546LV00001B/1/P

9 781939 654434